This Christmas planner

Belongs to:

_____

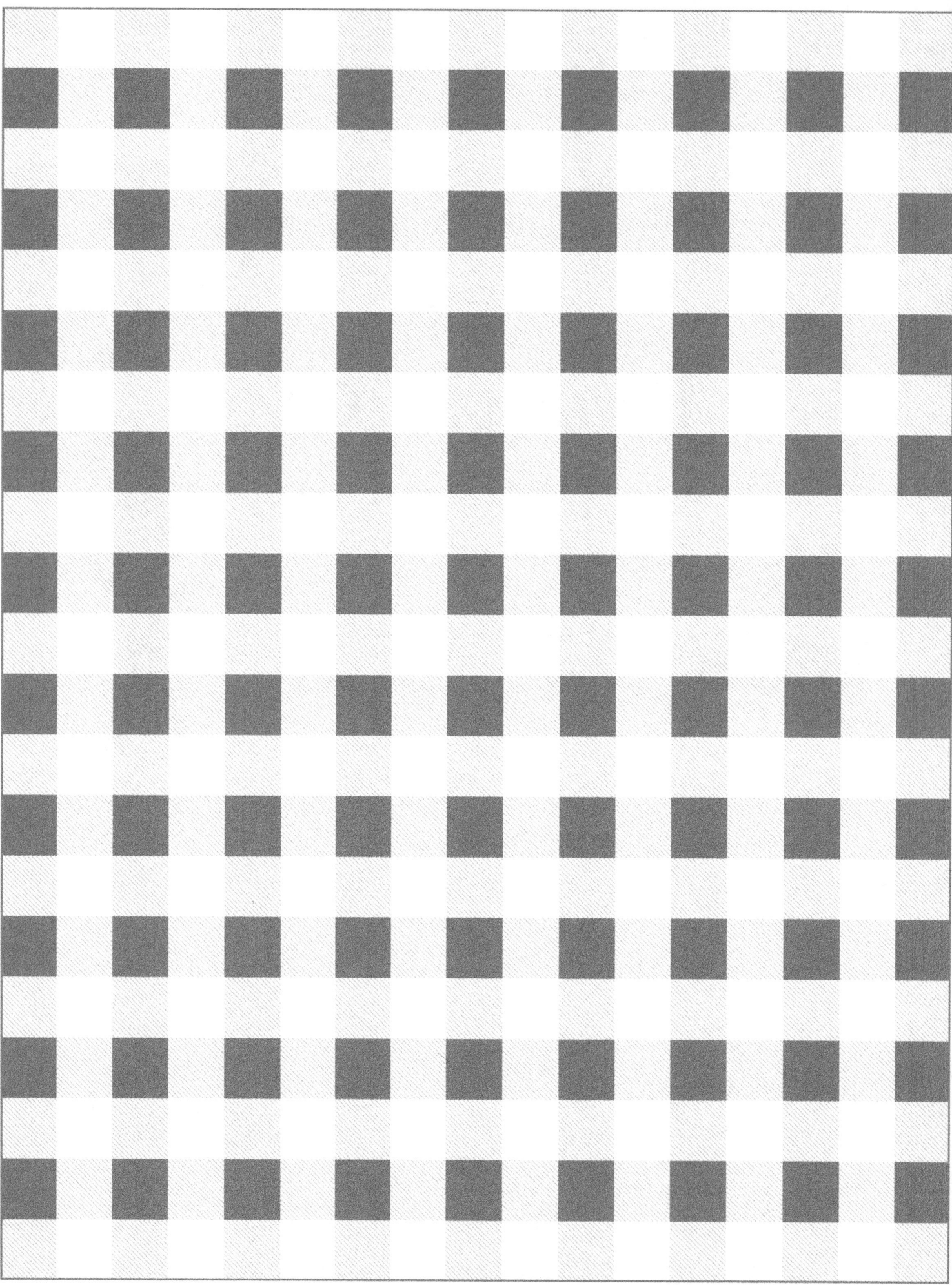

Dedication

This Christmas Planner Journal Log book is dedicated to all the holiday enthusiasts out there who love Christmas, love planning for the holidays, and want to document in the process.

You are my inspiration for producing books and I'm honored to be a part of keeping all of your Christmas planning notes and records organized.

This journal notebook will help you record your details about planning for the Christmas season.

Thoughtfully put together with these sections to record:

December Calendar, Master To-Do List, Elf Antics Planning, Menu Planner, Gift Planner, Budget Tracker, Baking Planner, Party Planning, Shopping Planner, Goals, Journal Pages, Photo Pages and much, much more!

How to Use this Book

The purpose of this book is to keep all of your Christmas Holiday notes all in one place. It will help keep you organized.

This Christmas Planner Journal will allow you to accurately document every detail about the holidays. It's a great way to chart your course through a Merry Christmas.

Here are examples of the prompts for you to fill in and write about your experience in this book:

1. Contact Page - Write your name.
2. December Calendar Overview - Calendar at a glance so you never miss a thing.
3. Advent Calendar - Each day could have a Bible verse, prayer and/ or instructions where to find their goody.
4. Master To-Do List - Make your lists and check them twice. Blank for you to fill in all the things you need to do.
5. Elf Antics Pages - For writing your ideas for some trouble your pesky little Elf could get into.
6. Weekly & Daily Planner - Schedule your week and day in detail.
7. Weekly Menu Planner With Shopping List - Plan your meals for the week and create your shopping list for groceries.
8. Gift Planner & Budget Tracker - Track your gifts list and how much you spent.
9. Holiday Baking Planner - Write what you plan to bake this holiday season.
10. Christmas Bucket List - For writing the things you want to make sure you do. Includes indoor list and outdoor list.
11. Stocking Stuffer Planner - Write who the gifts are for, the item, and budget.
12. Christmas Eve Planner - For writing your schedule, to-do list, traditions, activities & entertainment, and your meals for the day.
13. Black Friday Planner - Make a list of the item, store, and price.
14. Cyber Monday Planner - Make a list of the item, website, and price.
15. Christmas Budget Tracker - Track the item, how much budgeted for, actual price, and the difference.
16. Family Goals - This could be a fun way to continue or start new family Christmas traditions. Write your goal, steps to achieve the goal, and date accomplished.
17. Journal Pages - Blank lined note to reflect on the holiday season. This will be a treasure of memories for years to come and look back on.
18. Photo Pages - Place to paste your favorite pictures/ photos.
19. Christmas Wish Lists - Space to record Favorites, Need, Want, Read and Wear.
20. Christmas Party Planner - Record all the details for your party.
21. Reminder Pages - Space to write what worked, what didn't, and any recipes.
22. Gifts Received Tracker - Track the gift item, who it's from, notes, and checkbox for thank you sent.
23. Christmas Cards Organizer - Space to record Name, and a checkbox for sent and received.
24. Reindeer Games Page - A fun game for kids to play.

Enjoy!

December

Sun	Mon	Tue	Wed	Thu	Fri	Sat

Things I *must* get done!

December

Sun	Mon	Tue	Wed	Thu	Fri	Sat

Things I *must* get done!

Advent calendar

1	2	3	4
5	6	7	8
9	10	11	12
13	14	15	16
17	18	19	20
21	22	23	24

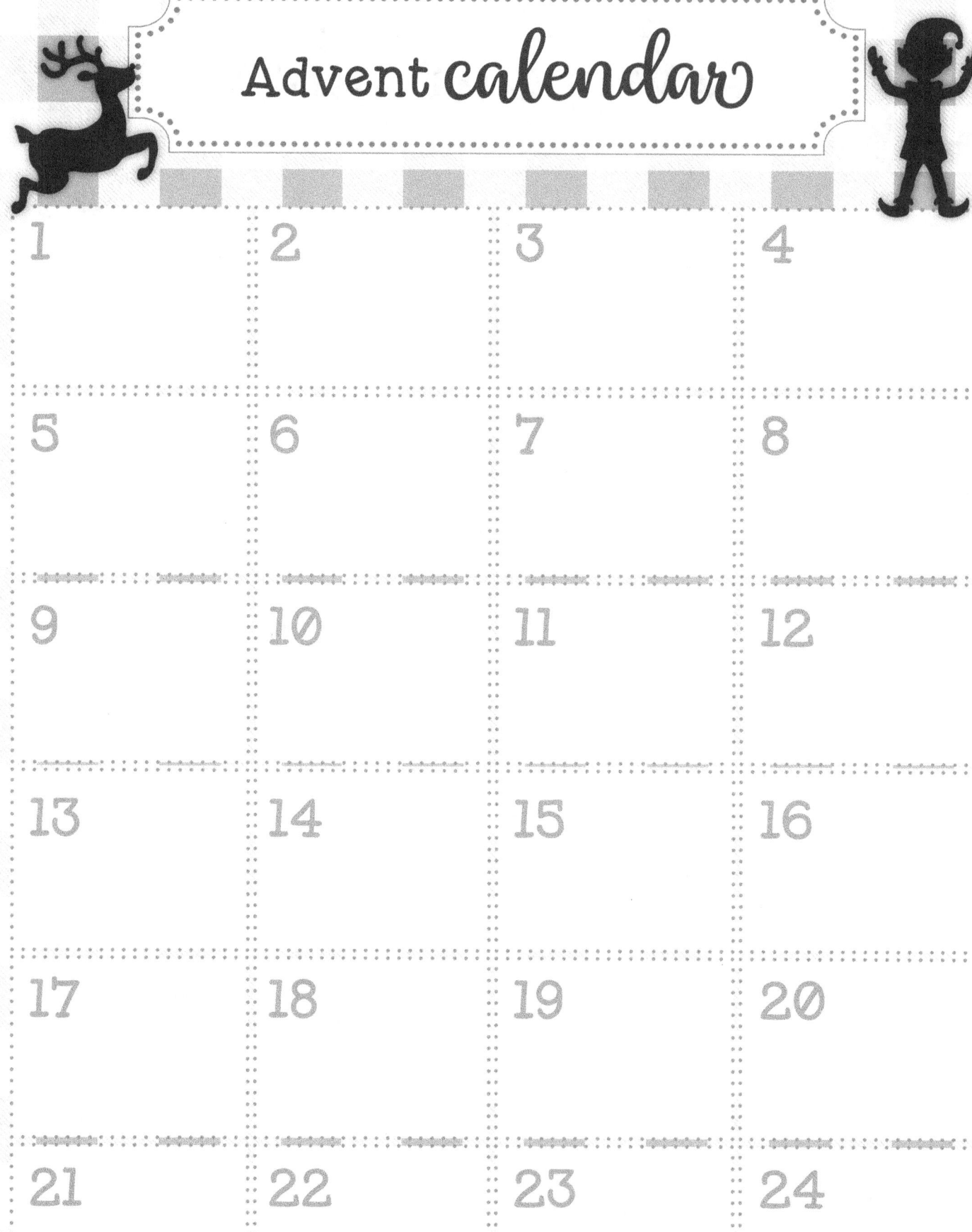

Master to-do list

Master to-do list

Master to-do list

Master to-do list

Weekly Planner

| Saturday |
| Friday |
| Thursday |
| Wednesday |
| Tuesday |
| Monday |
| Sunday |

weekly planner

Saturday	
Friday	
Thursday	
Wednesday	
Tuesday	
Monday	
Sunday	

Weekly planner

Day	
Saturday	
Friday	
Thursday	
Wednesday	
Tuesday	
Monday	
Sunday	

weekly planner

Saturday

Friday

Thursday

Wednesday

Tuesday

Monday

Sunday

weekly planner

Saturday	
Friday	
Thursday	
Wednesday	
Tuesday	
Monday	
Sunday	

Weekly planner

Saturday	
Friday	
Thursday	
Wednesday	
Tuesday	
Monday	
Sunday	

Daily planner

Daily Schedule

08:00

09:00

10:00

11:00

12:00

01:00

02:00

03:00

04:00

05:00

06:00

07:00

To Do

-
-
-
-
-
-
-
-
-
-
-
-
-
-
-

Top Five Priorities

Notes

Daily planner

Daily Schedule

08:00
09:00
10:00
11:00
12:00
01:00
02:00
03:00
04:00
05:00
06:00
07:00

To Do

○
○
○
○
○
○
○
○
○
○
○
○
○
○
○

Top Five Priorities

Notes

Daily planner

Daily Schedule

08:00
09:00
10:00
11:00
12:00
01:00
02:00
03:00
04:00
05:00
06:00
07:00

To Do

Top Five Priorities

Notes

Daily planner

Daily Schedule

- 08:00
- 09:00
- 10:00
- 11:00
- 12:00
- 01:00
- 02:00
- 03:00
- 04:00
- 05:00
- 06:00
- 07:00

To Do

- ○
- ○
- ○
- ○
- ○
- ○
- ○
- ○
- ○
- ○
- ○
- ○
- ○
- ○
- ○

Top Five Priorities

Notes

Daily planner

Daily Schedule | To Do

08:00

09:00

10:00

11:00

12:00

01:00

02:00

03:00

04:00

05:00

06:00

07:00

Top Five Priorities

Notes

Daily planner

Daily Schedule

08:00
09:00
10:00
11:00
12:00
01:00
02:00
03:00
04:00
05:00
06:00
07:00

To Do

○
○
○
○
○
○
○
○
○
○
○
○
○
○
○

Top Five Priorities

Notes

Daily planner

Daily Schedule

08:00
09:00
10:00
11:00
12:00
01:00
02:00
03:00
04:00
05:00
06:00
07:00

To Do

Top Five Priorities

Notes

Daily planner

Daily Schedule

- 08:00
- 09:00
- 10:00
- 11:00
- 12:00
- 01:00
- 02:00
- 03:00
- 04:00
- 05:00
- 06:00
- 07:00

To Do

Top Five Priorities

Notes

Daily planner

Daily Schedule

- 08:00
- 09:00
- 10:00
- 11:00
- 12:00
- 01:00
- 02:00
- 03:00
- 04:00
- 05:00
- 06:00
- 07:00

To Do

- ○
- ○
- ○
- ○
- ○
- ○
- ○
- ○
- ○
- ○
- ○
- ○
- ○
- ○

Top Five Priorities

Notes

Daily planner

Daily Schedule

- 08:00
- 09:00
- 10:00
- 11:00
- 12:00
- 01:00
- 02:00
- 03:00
- 04:00
- 05:00
- 06:00
- 07:00

To Do

- ○
- ○
- ○
- ○
- ○
- ○
- ○
- ○
- ○
- ○
- ○
- ○
- ○
- ○
- ○

Top Five Priorities

Notes

Daily planner

Daily Schedule

08:00
09:00
10:00
11:00
12:00
01:00
02:00
03:00
04:00
05:00
06:00
07:00

To Do

Top Five Priorities

Notes

Daily planner

Daily Schedule

08:00

09:00

10:00

11:00

12:00

01:00

02:00

03:00

04:00

05:00

06:00

07:00

To Do

-
-
-
-
-
-
-
-
-
-
-
-
-
-
-

Top Five Priorities

Notes

Daily planner

Daily Schedule

- 08:00
- 09:00
- 10:00
- 11:00
- 12:00
- 01:00
- 02:00
- 03:00
- 04:00
- 05:00
- 06:00
- 07:00

To Do

- ○
- ○
- ○
- ○
- ○
- ○
- ○
- ○
- ○
- ○
- ○
- ○
- ○
- ○

Top Five Priorities

Notes

Daily planner

Daily Schedule

- 08:00
- 09:00
- 10:00
- 11:00
- 12:00
- 01:00
- 02:00
- 03:00
- 04:00
- 05:00
- 06:00
- 07:00

To Do

- ○
- ○
- ○
- ○
- ○
- ○
- ○
- ○
- ○
- ○
- ○
- ○
- ○
- ○
- ○

Top Five Priorities

Notes

Menu planner

This Week's Meals

Monday

Tuesday

Wednesday

Thursday

Friday

Saturday

Sunday

Shopping List

Menu planner

This Week's Meals

Monday

Tuesday

Wednesday

Thursday

Friday

Saturday

Sunday

Shopping List

Menu planner

This Week's Meals

Monday

Tuesday

Wednesday

Thursday

Friday

Saturday

Sunday

Shopping List

Menu planner

This Week's Meals

Monday

Tuesday

Wednesday

Thursday

Friday

Saturday

Sunday

Shopping List

Menu planner

This Week's Meals

Monday

Tuesday

Wednesday

Thursday

Friday

Saturday

Sunday

Shopping List

Menu planner

This Week's Meals

Monday

Tuesday

Wednesday

Thursday

Friday

Saturday

Sunday

Shopping List

Menu planner

This Week's Meals

Monday

Tuesday

Wednesday

Thursday

Friday

Saturday

Sunday

Shopping List

Gift planner

Name	Gift	Budget	✓
			☐
			☐
			☐
			☐
			☐
			☐
			☐
			☐
			☐
			☐
			☐
			☐
			☐
			☐
			☐
			☐
			☐
			☐
			☐
			☐
			☐

Gift planner

Name	Gift	Budget	✓
			☐
			☐
			☐
			☐
			☐
			☐
			☐
			☐
			☐
			☐
			☐
			☐
			☐
			☐
			☐
			☐
			☐
			☐
			☐
			☐
			☐

Gift planner

Name	Gift	Budget	✓
			☐
			☐
			☐
			☐
			☐
			☐
			☐
			☐
			☐
			☐
			☐
			☐
			☐
			☐
			☐
			☐
			☐
			☐
			☐
			☐
			☐

Gift planner

Name	Gift	Budget	✓
			☐
			☐
			☐
			☐
			☐
			☐
			☐
			☐
			☐
			☐
			☐
			☐
			☐
			☐
			☐
			☐
			☐
			☐
			☐

Gift planner

Name	Gift	Budget	✓
			☐
			☐
			☐
			☐
			☐
			☐
			☐
			☐
			☐
			☐
			☐
			☐
			☐
			☐
			☐
			☐
			☐
			☐
			☐
			☐
			☐
			☐

Holiday Baking planner

Recipe Name	Source & Page #	Yield

Special ingredients to buy

Special Event to Bake For

Holiday Baking planner

Recipe Name	Source & Page #	Yield

Special ingredients to buy

Special Event to Bake For

Holiday Baking planner

Recipe Name	Source & Page #	Yield

Special ingredients to buy

Special Event to Bake For

Holiday Baking planner

Recipe Name	Source & Page #	Yield

Special ingredients to buy

Special Event to Bake For

Christmas Bucket List

Indoor	Outdoor
☐	☐
☐	☐
☐	☐
☐	☐
☐	☐
☐	☐
☐	☐
☐	☐
☐	☐
☐	☐
☐	☐
☐	☐
☐	☐
☐	☐
☐	☐
☐	☐
☐	☐

Christmas Bucket list

Indoor	Outdoor
☐	☐
☐	☐
☐	☐
☐	☐
☐	☐
☐	☐
☐	☐
☐	☐
☐	☐
☐	☐
☐	☐
☐	☐
☐	☐
☐	☐
☐	☐
☐	☐
☐	☐

Christmas Bucket list

Indoor	Outdoor
☐	☐
☐	☐
☐	☐
☐	☐
☐	☐
☐	☐
☐	☐
☐	☐
☐	☐
☐	☐
☐	☐
☐	☐
☐	☐
☐	☐
☐	☐
☐	☐
☐	☐
☐	☐

Christmas Bucket list

Indoor	Outdoor
☐	☐
☐	☐
☐	☐
☐	☐
☐	☐
☐	☐
☐	☐
☐	☐
☐	☐
☐	☐
☐	☐
☐	☐
☐	☐
☐	☐
☐	☐
☐	☐
☐	☐
☐	☐

Christmas Bucket List

Indoor	Outdoor
☐	☐

Stocking Stuffer planner

Name:	
Stuffers	Budget

Name:	
Stuffers	Budget

Name:	
Stuffers	Budget

Name:	
Stuffers	Budget

Name:	
Stuffers	Budget

Name:	
Stuffers	Budget

Stocking Stuffer planner

Name: _____

Stuffers	Budget

Name: _____

Stuffers	Budget

Name: _____

Stuffers	Budget

Name: _____

Stuffers	Budget

Name: _____

Stuffers	Budget

Name: _____

Stuffers	Budget

Christmas Eve planner

Today's Schedule

Traditions

Activities & Entertainment

To Do List

Breakfast

Lunch

Dinner

Christmas Eve planner

Today's Schedule

Traditions

Activities & Entertainment

To Do List

Breakfast

Lunch

Dinner

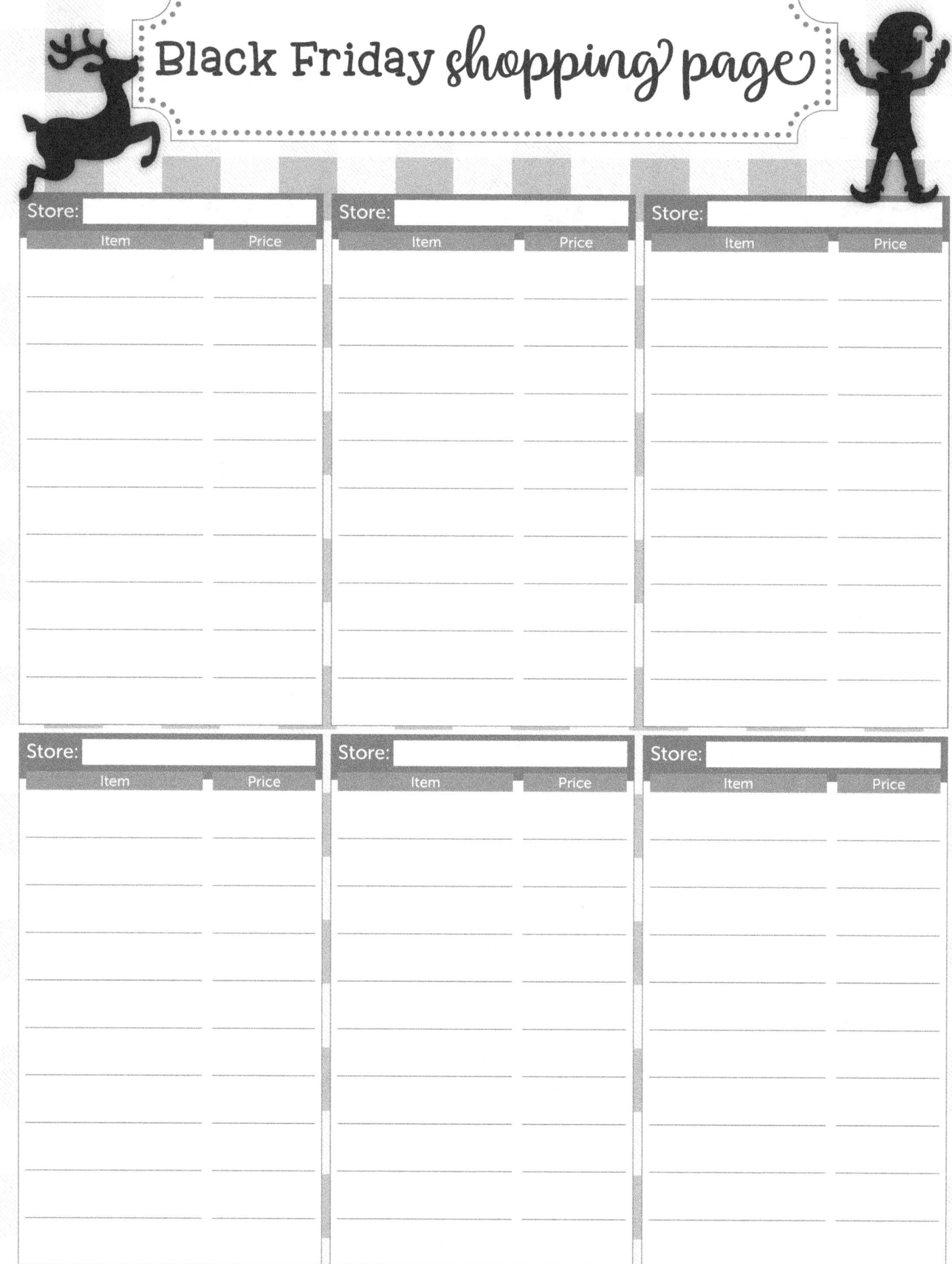

Black Friday shopping page

Store:		Store:		Store:	
Item	Price	Item	Price	Item	Price

Store:		Store:		Store:	
Item	Price	Item	Price	Item	Price

Christmas budget tracker

Item	Budgeted	Actual	Difference
Total			

Christmas budget tracker

Item	Budgeted	Actual	Difference
Total			

Christmas budget tracker

Item	Budgeted	Actual	Difference
Total			

Christmas budget tracker

Item	Budgeted	Actual	Difference
Total			

Christmas budget tracker

Item	Budgeted	Actual	Difference
Total			

Family goals

Goal	Steps to reach our goal

Accomplished Date:

Goal	Steps to reach our goal

Accomplished Date:

Goal	Steps to reach our goal

Accomplished Date:

Goal	Steps to reach our goal

Accomplished Date:

Date:

Family goals

Goal	Steps to reach our goal

Accomplished Date:

Goal	Steps to reach our goal

Accomplished Date:

Goal	Steps to reach our goal

Accomplished Date:

Goal	Steps to reach our goal

Accomplished Date:

Journal

Date:

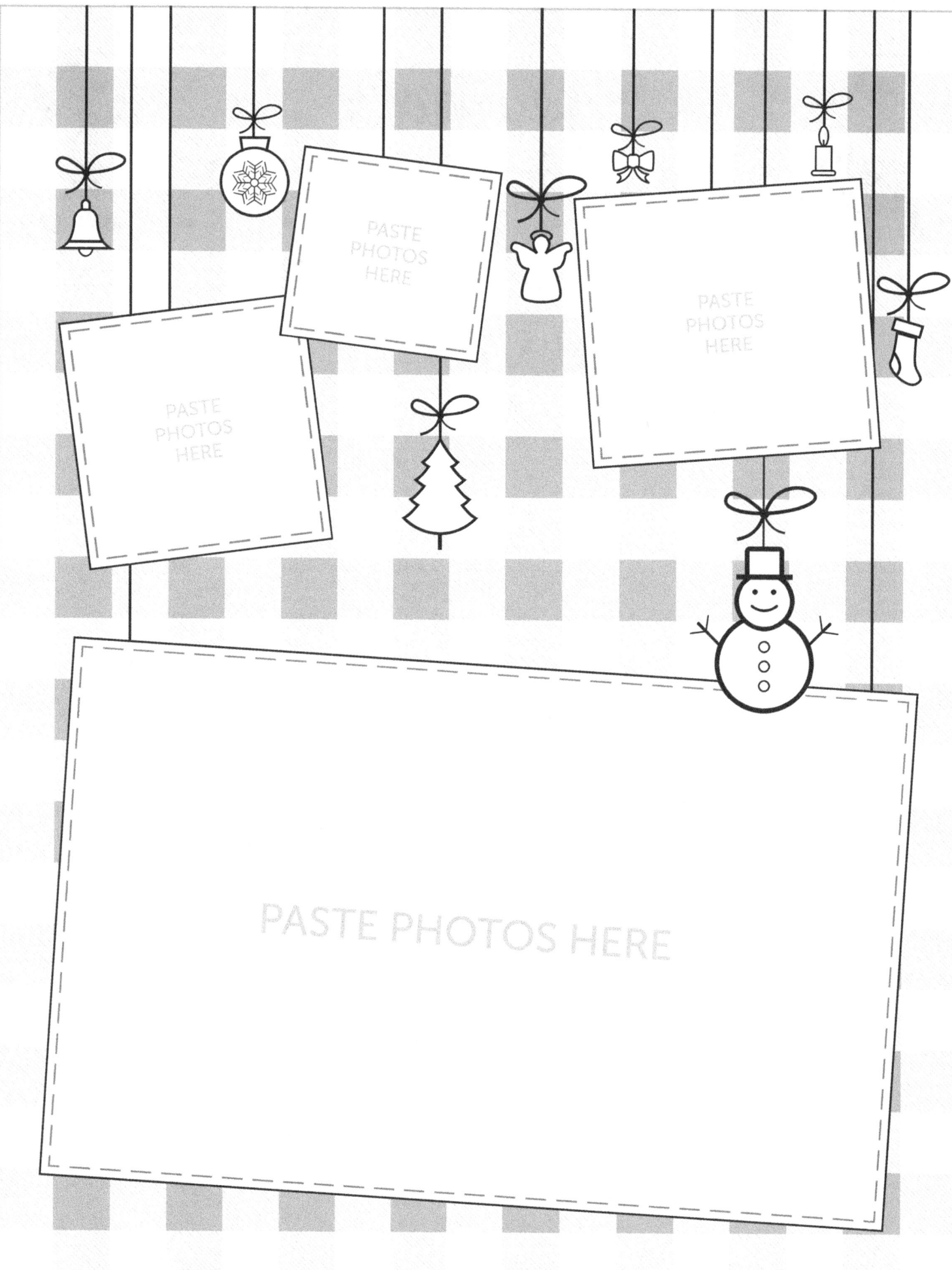

Family goals

Goal	Steps to reach our goal
Accomplished Date:	
Goal	Steps to reach our goal
Accomplished Date:	
Goal	Steps to reach our goal
Accomplished Date:	
Goal	Steps to reach our goal
Accomplished Date:	

Journal

Date:

Family goals

Goal	Steps to reach our goal

Accomplished Date:

Goal	Steps to reach our goal

Accomplished Date:

Goal	Steps to reach our goal

Accomplished Date:

Goal	Steps to reach our goal

Accomplished Date:

Journal

Date:

Family goals

Goal	Steps to reach our goal

Accomplished Date:

Goal	Steps to reach our goal

Accomplished Date:

Goal	Steps to reach our goal

Accomplished Date:

Goal	Steps to reach our goal

Accomplished Date:

Journal

Date:

Christmas Wish list

Favorites

Need

Want

Read

Wear

Christmas Wish list

Favorites

Need

Want

Read

Wear

Christmas party planner

Event:

Date: Time:

Location:

Backup location:

- ☐ Reserve venue
- ☐ Send invitations
- ☐ Plan food
- ☐ Plan activities
- ☐ Plan decor

ATTENDEES

Name	Address	Invited	RSVP'd

PARTY SCHEDULE

Time	Activity	Notes

Reminder page

What worked?	What didn't?	Favorite recipes

Christmas party planner

Event: _____

Date: _____ Time: _____

Location: _____

Backup location: _____

- ☐ Reserve venue
- ☐ Send invitations
- ☐ Plan food
- ☐ Plan activities
- ☐ Plan decor

ATTENDEES

Name	Address	Invited	RSVP'd

PARTY SCHEDULE

Time	Activity	Notes

Reminder page

What worked?	What didn't?	Favorite recipes

Journal

Date:

Christmas party planner

Event: _____

Date: _____ Time: _____

Location: _____

Backup location: _____

- ☐ Reserve venue
- ☐ Send invitations
- ☐ Plan food
- ☐ Plan activities
- ☐ Plan decor

ATTENDEES

Name	Address	Invited	RSVP'd

PARTY SCHEDULE

Time	Activity	Notes

Reminder page

What worked?	What didn't?	Favorite recipes

Date:

Christmas party planner

Event: _____

Date: _____ Time: _____

Location: _____

Backup location: _____

☐ Reserve venue
☐ Send invitations
☐ Plan food
☐ Plan activities
☐ Plan decor

ATTENDEES

Name	Address	Invited	RSVP'd

PARTY SCHEDULE

Time	Activity	Notes

Reminder page

What worked?	What didn't?	Favorite recipes

Journal

Date:

Received gift tracker

Gift	From	Notes	Thank You Sent

Received gift tracker

Gift	From	Notes	Thank You Sent

Card Organizer

Name	Sent?	Received?
	☐	☐
	☐	☐
	☐	☐
	☐	☐
	☐	☐
	☐	☐
	☐	☐
	☐	☐
	☐	☐
	☐	☐
	☐	☐
	☐	☐
	☐	☐
	☐	☐
	☐	☐
	☐	☐
	☐	☐
	☐	☐
	☐	☐
	☐	☐

Card Organizer

Name	Sent?	Received?
	☐	☐
	☐	☐
	☐	☐
	☐	☐
	☐	☐
	☐	☐
	☐	☐
	☐	☐
	☐	☐
	☐	☐
	☐	☐
	☐	☐
	☐	☐
	☐	☐
	☐	☐
	☐	☐
	☐	☐
	☐	☐
	☐	☐
	☐	☐
	☐	☐

Elf antics

Ideas

Supply List

Elf antics

Ideas	Supply List

Elf antics

Ideas	Supply List

Reindeer games

_____	He'll be dressed in a tutu.	Blitzen
_____	He considers himself Spanish royalty.	Dasher
_____	Always trying to be the match maker.	Comet
_____	Has a second job as a linebacker.	Prancer
_____	First Reindeer to learn hip hop.	Cupid
_____	You'd find him cleaning your bathroom.	Donner
_____	Plays mean tricks on the elves.	Vixen
_____	The fastest of them all.	Dancer
_____	Considered the most aggressive of all the reindeer.	Comet
_____	Considers himself very stylish	Prancer
_____	Always wants Santa to fly in an egg shaped pattern.	Cupid
_____	He'll light the way through the fog.	Dancer
_____	Always on his hind legs trying to impress Santa.	Rudolph
_____	His second favorite holiday is Valentine's Day.	Dasher
_____	The others consider his pompous gait a little irritating.	Blitzen

Reminder page

What worked?	What didn't?	Favorite recipes

Reminder page

What worked?	What didn't?	Favorite recipes

Reminder page

What worked?	What didn't?	Favorite recipes

Reminder page

What worked?	What didn't?	Favorite recipes

Reminder page

What worked?	What didn't?	Favorite recipes

Reminder page

What worked?	What didn't?	Favorite recipes

Journal

Date:

Journal

Date:

Journal

Date:

Journal

Date:

Journal

Date:

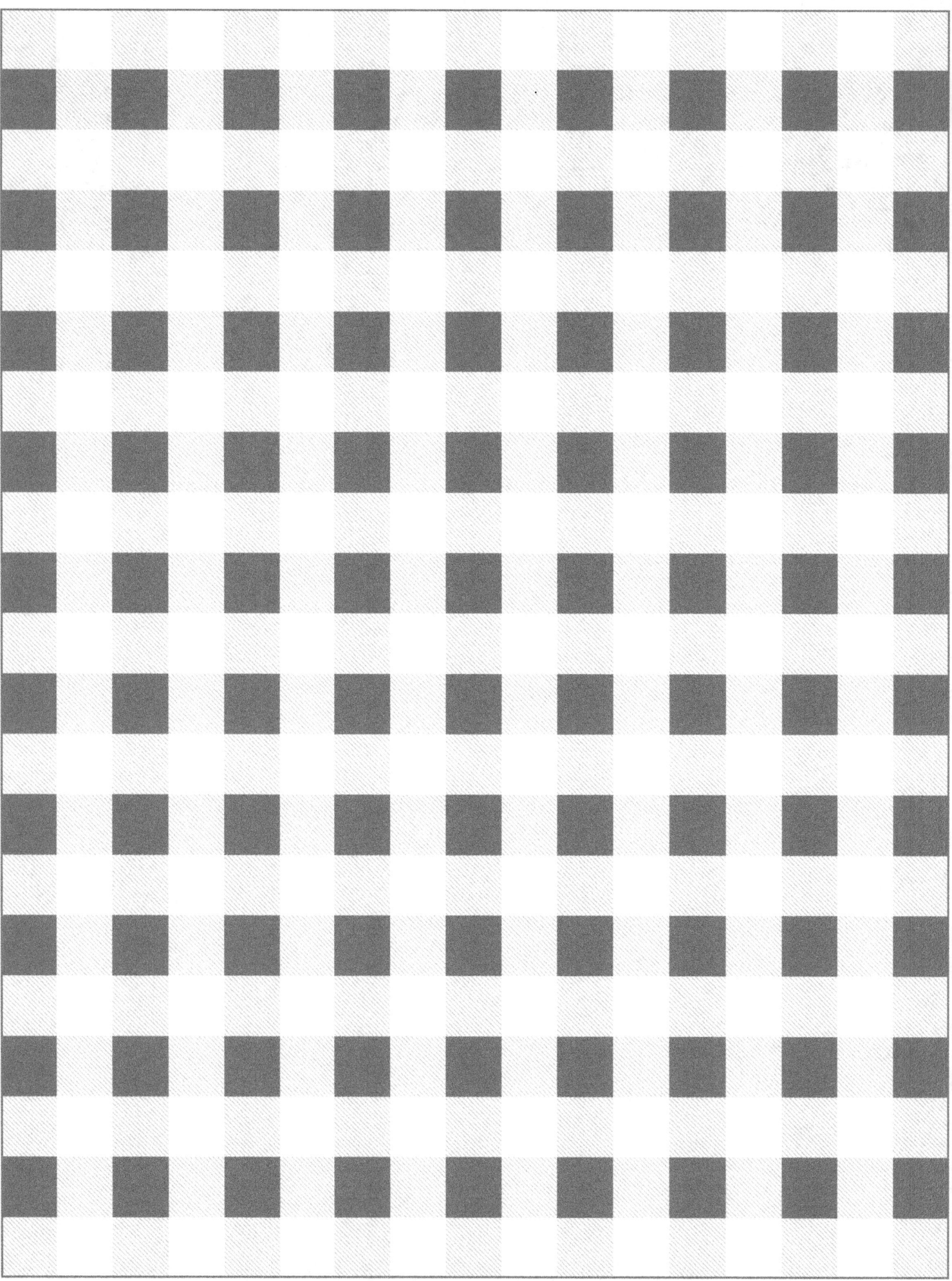

www.ingramcontent.com/pod-product-compliance
Lightning Source LLC
Chambersburg PA
CBHW081230080526
44587CB00022B/3887